40 Prayers for My Husband

Drawing near to God for the man you love.

by Selena Frederick

40
Prayers for
My Husband

Drawing near to God for the man you love.

Copyright © 2019 by Ryan and Selena Frederick

Published by Cormens Press, a division of Vilicus LLC

First Edition

Author portrait by Anje Haisch. Used with permission.

ISBN-10: 0-9974713-5-2

ISBN-13: 978-0-9974713-5-9

(pbk. bw.)

1 3 5 7 9 10 8 6 4 2   22 21 20 19 18

Printed in the United States of America

To Mom, my first and forever prayer warrior

Contents

Introduction

If you're reading this book, then you've decided to begin a journey of prayer for your husband (yeah!). Maybe you're excited to get started, or maybe you don't really know where to begin, which is why you picked up this book. Either way, I'm grateful for the opportunity to journey with you.

Writing this book has personally been a joy-filled task because it's forced me to sit and be in the presence of my King. Spending time communing with God, about the one person on earth who is my closest friend and covenant partner, has brought me so much hope—I pray you experience the true joy and deep hope that comes from being in his presence.

As you get started, I'd love to share with you a few things God has taught me through this book, and I pray that you find it both encouraging and maybe even a bit challenging—in the best way!

The Gift of Prayer

First things first, prayer is a privilege that was made available to us through the person and work of Jesus Christ. If we look back through the Old Testament, before Christ came to earth, only a high priest could enter the throne room to petition and commune with God on behalf of the people. Jesus' death on the cross changed everything! It tore the veil and cleared the way for us to pray/speak directly to God. Prayer is truly a gift!

Hebrews 4 teaches us that Jesus is our high priest, and he not only empathizes with us in our struggles and pain, but when we enter the throne room, we are met with his grace and mercy—not because of anything we have done, but because of who Jesus is and the work he completed. He secured our salvation and the grace we desperately needed so that we could pray and commune with God. This is good news! As we pray, let's remind our hearts of what it cost to be in this holy place.

Less Striving, More Being

Secondly, being in his presence and praying to him has taught me how prayer is less about me striving to say or do the right thing and more about me being still and knowing him.

The more I spend time getting to know God, the more my heart is transformed by him. Psalm 46:10 encourages us to be still and know that he is God. So much of understanding how to commune with God begins with knowing God and understanding his character.

One primary way we get to know God is through spending time in his Word. There is no substitute for spending time reading, praying, and absorbing the Bible. That is one of the primary reasons why you will find each daily prayer in this book intertwined with scripture. Not to name and claim any sort of power that does not belong to us, but rather to remind our hearts of the One who is all-powerful, never changing, and ever present—the King of kings!

Talking to and communing with our holy God whenever and wherever we want is one of the greatest blessings he's given us. Over the past two decades, God has graciously helped me understand that blessings require a kind of tending once received. For years I thought blessings were all about receiving and that was the end of it. But God continues to show me that his gifts are greater and go so much further than just receiving them. If you take a moment to stop and think about all the blessings in your life (e.g. your spouse, children, job, home, etc.), each of them requires consistent care and attention in order for proper function and growth to happen. To be clear, we are not the ones who cause or create growth; only God is. He has entrusted us to faithfully steward and care for the blessings he's given us. The same is true for prayer. It's often in the midst of what I'll call "blessing tending" when we experience our own sanctification. As prayer is a blessing, I would encourage you to tend to it well! Stay committed to the process and remember the purpose and gift that prayer is.

Intentionally Present

Lastly, building a vibrant prayer life takes intentionality. To get the most out of this book, I encourage you to truly *participate*. What I mean is that when you sit down to pray, be fully present, without distraction, completely transparent—surrendered. It's when we are in this posture of total surrender that we are better able to follow Jesus and pray as he did.

In Matthew 6:5–15, better known as the Lord's Prayer, Jesus instructs us how and even where to pray—they are deeply intertwined. He says not to pray where everyone can see, but rather in secret. Why? There are probably many reasons for Jesus' instruction, but I believe one thing God is asking of us is to take steps toward being fully known rather than being on display. This was a hard concept to grasp two thousand years ago as well as today. But I have faith in the Holy Spirit to empower you as you surrender and commune with God. Trust him and be vulnerable. As we have learned through his Word, he is trustworthy!

Talking to God is intimate, sacred, and powerful. Communing with the Creator of the universe should elicit some level of fearful, humble respect and not simply our list of wants and needs. I am saying this to myself more than anyone else. Too many times I've failed and come to God listing off everything I need and want, especially when it comes to my marriage and my husband. And while he is present with me in these selfish prayers, he desires so much more for me than a simple answer to my requests and needs. He wants me to know him, trust him, and allow him to transform my life from the inside out.

As you dive into the next forty days, I would like to assure and encourage you to pray vulnerably, transparently, and without distraction. Let your guard down, draw near to God, and allow him to draw near to you. I would like to take a moment to pray for you, Fierce Wife, as you get started on your prayer journey.

Why 40 Days?

You may be wondering about the duration of this book. As it turns out, there's just something special about the number *40*. The main reason we chose 40 days was in hopes that it would help you establish a new, lasting habit of prayer—research shows that it takes between four and eight weeks to create a new, worthwhile habit. But that's just part of the story.

Ryan and I also enjoy the fact that the number 40 is a theme seen in the Bible that reminds us of God's goodness. Moses was on Mount Sinai for 40 days and 40 nights (Exodus 24:18), Jesus spent 40 days and 40 nights in the desert, being tested (Matthew 4:2), there were 40 days between Jesus' resurrection and ascension (Acts 1:3), and other occurrences of 40.

We don't intend to place too much emphasis on some hidden meaning or secret to be unlocked by the number 40. It's not magical or mystical. We simply view it as a sweet reminder of God's sovereignty and grace as often seen in the passages and events where the number happens to be included.

To make things flexible, every seventh day is designated as a *rest and reflect day*. Use it at your discretion. Feel free to catch up on missed days, journal, or spend extra time with your husband—it's your call. I do recommend quietly reflecting on the past week as well as the day's passage for a few minutes, then write down anything that comes to mind. You will never regret spending time being still and knowing who God is.

With that said, onward! I hope the next forty days enliven your relationship with God and enrich your relationship with your husband. I'm praying for you, friend. Stay fierce!

Jesus, I praise and thank you for who you are and for meeting us where we are. Thank you for the blessing of prayer and for clearing the way for us to be able to pray for our husbands for the next forty days. I ask for openness in the heart of the wife reading this, no matter what she is facing in her marriage. I pray that the work you accomplish in and through her over the next forty days would be undeniable and complete evidence of you! Be her strength and give her the courage to say yes to spending time communing with you, especially when that means saying no to other things. May her heart be reminded of the purpose and power of prayer.

Let your presence overwhelm her soul as she contends for the heart, mind, body, and soul of her husband. Your word assures us that you hear our prayers, and so I ask that she would find rest, peace, and confidence in the fact that her prayers don't require striving, but rather resting.

In Jesus' name, amen.

Taking Inventory

Every journey must have a destination in mind, but to know that, you must also know your starting point. Answer the questions below as honestly and specifically as you can. Then, watch and see what God does.

List some ways you have prayed for your husband currently or in the past.

What's on your husband's heart right now that you could pray for?

How would you like to grow in praying for your husband?

What difference do you think it could make in your marriage if you and your husband prayed for each other daily?

How are you praying God will move in your life and in your marriage over the next forty days? Be specific.

On a scale of 1 to 10, how would you rate the following areas of your marriage? (1 = Terrible, 10 = Great)

Overall Marital Unity, Health, and Enjoyment

| 1 | 2 | 3 | 4 | 5 | 6 | 7 | 8 | 9 | 10 |

Communication

| 1 | 2 | 3 | 4 | 5 | 6 | 7 | 8 | 9 | 10 |

Handling Conflict

| 1 | 2 | 3 | 4 | 5 | 6 | 7 | 8 | 9 | 10 |

Emotional Intimacy

| 1 | 2 | 3 | 4 | 5 | 6 | 7 | 8 | 9 | 10 |

Sexual Intimacy

| 1 | 2 | 3 | 4 | 5 | 6 | 7 | 8 | 9 | 10 |

Unity in Finances

| 1 | 2 | 3 | 4 | 5 | 6 | 7 | 8 | 9 | 10 |

Heads up: At the end of the book, you will be prompted to return to this page and revisit your ratings above. At that time, circle your new numbers with a different-colored ink to get an idea of how God has worked in your marriage over the course of your 40-day journey.

Remember the Whole Way

And you shall
remember the whole way
that the Lord your God has led
you these forty years in the
wilderness.

_____

Deuteronomy 8:2

As you venture forth, use this area to quickly jot down instances when God answers prayer. Include dates and details. Refer back to it often to remind yourself of God's faithfulness.

Day 1
For Freedom

For freedom Christ has set us free; stand firm therefore, and do not submit again to a yoke of slavery.

Galatians 5:1

Jesus, thank you for coming to earth to deliver us from sin and eternal separation from you. It is for freedom you set us free, and it is only through you that we can stand firm and live in freedom. Your life, death, and resurrection released us from the chains of self-reliance and slavery to idols. I praise you for consistently bringing me to a place of freedom. Thank you for your love that reaches to the heavens, and for your faithfulness that stretches to the skies (Psalm 36:5).

Help me to share your goodness and the message of your freedom with the world, beginning with my husband. I pray that he would find and experience true freedom in you, specifically in the midst of his daily struggles with sin. God, I ask for you to illuminate your steadfast love to my husband's soul. Help him to see struggles not as points of defeat, but holy places of sanctification because of you. I pray he would find encouragement in his struggles and he wouldn't simply want to escape them. In your Word you remind us that we will have trials in this life, but you have already overcome the world!

As we learn to live in freedom and in light of the gospel, you don't leave us alone. Rather, you promise to never leave or forsake us(Hebrews 13:5) Bring my husband and me into your freedom step-by-step. May we be reminded of your unrestrained mercy (Psalm 40:11) that has delivered us from self-reliance into God reliance. Help us to experience true freedom that is only found in you.

In Jesus' name, amen.

I pray that Erik may continue to see and know your grace, and that I can be a giver of God's grace and peace and hope for him. In times of struggle, for him or me, I pray that I may turn to you for guidance and love, to better love and serve you, and to better love Erik. Amen.

Day 2
For Overwhelming Peace

"Peace I leave with you; my peace I give to you. Not as the world gives do I give to you. Let not your hearts be troubled, neither let them be afraid."

_____

John 14:27

Jesus, thank you for coming down to us. For paving the way and clearing the path for us to know you and receive all that you have for us. You didn't have to, and still you chose to live among us—to teach us your ways so we could find and receive spiritual fruit, such as peace that is unaffected by our current circumstances. Thank you that you didn't leave us alone, but gave us a Helper and Advocate to minister your peace to our hearts when fear and anxiety try to take up residence. I ask you to anchor our souls in you.

I humbly ask you, God, that when my husband faces trials and feels the need to look elsewhere to find peace in this world through distractions or idols claiming to bring peace—please, God, help him to fix his eyes on you and not on himself. May he be reminded of your deep peace that is not of this world (Philippians 4:7). A peace that can only be explained and found in you. Help him to know and live in your peace that surpasses all understanding. I pray that he would find freedom in your peace and be assured of it guarding his heart and mind.

As my husband and I continue to grow in our understanding and experience of your peace in our marriage (Matthew 5:9), I pray that we would also share our experiences with the world. May the peace we experience in our marriage be evidence of you, and above all, may it reflect your glory. Thank you, Jesus, for your undeserved peace that goes beyond our understanding. To our Prince of Peace—we give you all the glory.

In Jesus' name, amen.

**Use these pages to journal your thoughts,
write your own prayer, or both.**

Date _____

Day 3
For a Community of Brothers

As soon as he had finished speaking to Saul, the soul of Jonathan was knit to the soul of David, and Jonathan loved him as his own soul.

_____

1 Samuel 18:1

Thank you, Father, that you are a relational God, and you desire us to experience the beauty of friendship the way you intended it. When you are at the center of our friendships, they flourish. There is nothing we can't get through, because your higher ways govern and preserve us, and in choosing you as the governing authority in our friendship, we are choosing freedom. It's in these friendships where we can speak the truth in love and be honest and fully known (Ephesians 4:15). You never created us to be alone, but for relationship.

I graciously ask you to bring covenant friendships into my husband's life. I pray that he would desire to have a band of spiritual brothers who would want to know him and that he would want to be known by. You brought David and Jonathan together—knitting their souls in a most holy way. I ask that you would please bring a David or a Jonathan into his life. Someone who cares about the present state of his soul as well as the future state. May you knit their souls together in a way that brings glory to you.

I praise you and thank you for the friends you have already blessed us with. May they be ones who aren't afraid to ask us the hard questions in order to sharpen (Proverbs 27:17) us and bring us back to you when necessary. Help us to never idolize our friends, but to be honest with them and available for them. Open our eyes and our hearts to recognize and nurture these friendships.

In Jesus' name, amen.

Use these pages to journal your thoughts, write your own prayer, or both.

Date _____

Day 4
For Unshakable and Multiplied Joy

But the fruit of the Spirit is love, joy, peace, patience, kindness, goodness, faithfulness, gentleness, self-control; against such things there is no law.

Galatians 5:22–23

Thank you, Holy Spirit, for being a God of joy! You are faithful to produce it in us when we trust and live in you (Galatians 5:25). The assurance of knowing our eternal hope is secure in you produces a deep joy that we can't help but share—and in turn it is organically multiplied. God, help us to understand and value the joy that we have in you for what it is: a product—a fruit produced because of your presence in our lives. The joy we have in you provides us strength every day!

Holy Spirit, I ask that you would draw the heart of my husband deeper into you. I pray that as he knows you more, he would experience unshakable, multiplied joy. I pray that throughout his day he would be so deeply rooted in you that your joy would overflow wherever he goes. May his joy be multiplied in a noticeable way by others around him. Help him to freely share the joy he has, despite the circumstances he might be experiencing. I pray that your message of hope, love, and grace would excite him like the man in the parable who sold everything to buy the field that held the treasure (Matthew 13:44). May your joy lead his every move, motivate his thoughts, and multiply in his heart.

Thank you for your presence that never leaves or forsakes us but stays with us (Deuteronomy 31:6; Hebrews 13:5). When we abide in you, spiritual fruit is produced. Thank you for your faithful, transformative presence in our lives. We love you and thank you for the joy you have produced and will produce in our marriage.

In Jesus' name, amen.

Use these pages to journal your thoughts, write your own prayer, or both.

Date _____

33

Day 5
For Empathy and Compassion

Put on then, as God's chosen ones, holy and beloved, compassionate hearts, kindness, humility, meekness, and patience, bearing with one another and, if one has a complaint against another, forgiving each other; as the Lord has forgiven you, so you also must forgive.

Colossians 3:12–13

Father God, thank you for your compassion and empathy toward us, your children. The war between flesh and Spirit wages on inside the deepest parts of us, but you remain steadfast, good, and sovereign. Your love and forgiveness of our sin leads us to respond with compassion rather than anger—empathy instead of apathy. I praise you, Holy Spirit, for opening my heart and eyes to see my husband the way you do. Your grace is overwhelming and causes my soul to worship!

Lord, I ask you to help my husband put on empathy, despite the feelings of frustration he may feel toward me or his day. Your Word faithfully and consistently reminds us of your loving patience and how it bears with us in our shortcomings every day. Help him to respond to challenging situations as you have responded to us. The world shouts at him to say whatever he feels—even if it is unkind, impatient, and harsh to those around him. Again, I ask that you would fill him with compassion and empathy toward me, his family, and our community. Help him to stand firm and trust that your ways are higher. I ask that you would keep his heart soft toward you. Please, Jesus, teach us and help our hearts' first response to be compassionate and empathetic—despite our feelings or emotions in the moment.

Jesus, thank you for your compassionate response to humbly descend to earth and die for us. Your compassion toward us is immeasurable! Thank you for choosing us and for compassionately loving us enough to die—even while we were still sinners (Romans 5:8).

In Jesus' name, amen.

**Use these pages to journal your thoughts,
write your own prayer, or both.**

Date _____

Day 6
That He Would Know Perfect Love

So we have come to know and to believe the love that God has for us. God is love, and whoever abides in love abides in God, and God abides in him.

1 John 4:16

My God, thank you for being the unconditional lover of my soul, and that of my husband's. I praise you for being the creator and definition of love. Lead us into understanding the depths and functionality of your love in our lives and in our marriage. We have past associations with the idea of love that have caused hurt and fear. This has caused us to build up walls around our souls. We don't want to be fully known because we fear being hurt, especially by each other. Vulnerability feels like it comes at a price that our fear isn't willing to pay. Shatter the lies we believed about love that would keep us alone and unknown. Lord, help us in our unbelief. Help us to understand you and thus understand love.

Father, I pray that you would lead my husband's beliefs in what it means to be loved unconditionally and completely by you. I pray that your grace would lead him into knowing and experiencing your perfect love in his heart. I ask you, Father, that all his fears about being fully known and fully loved would fall by the wayside and that he would walk securely in your love. From here, I pray you would lead him in how he can love others.

Thank you, Jesus, for loving us first. It's only because of your love that we can love each other (1 John 4:19). Teach us how to abide in you and how your love can better abide in us. Let your love cast out our fears that may have ruled and fueled our understanding of love. Thank you, Father, for your perfect display of love to us through Jesus' death on the cross. Lead us to love each other as you have loved us: perfectly, selflessly, and without fear.

In Jesus' name, amen.

Use these pages to journal your thoughts, write your own prayer, or both.   Date _____

Day 7
Rest and Reflect

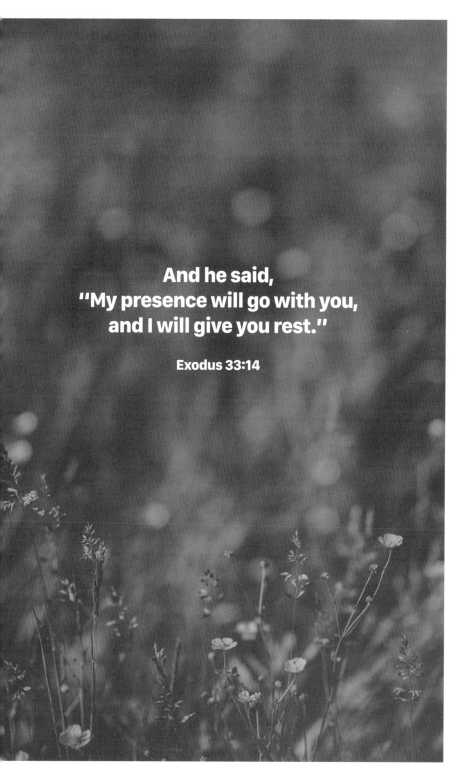

And he said,
"My presence will go with you,
and I will give you rest."

Exodus 33:14

Take time today to rest in who God is. Reflect on the prayers over the past week. Use the space below to record how God has been working in your heart and marriage.

Day 8
That He Would Walk in Patience

I therefore, a prisoner for the Lord, urge you
to walk in a manner worthy of the calling to
which you have been called, with all humility
and gentleness, with patience, bearing with
one another in love.

Ephesians 4:1–2

Holy Spirit, thank you for your presence, your counsel, and your love. It is by you and through you that eternal and holy fruit is produced. As I read your Word, you are so faithful to teach me about the process of growth and production. Growth requires a divine presence and power outside of ourselves. Only you can cause and create growth (1 Corinthians 3:6). You allow me to take part in the planting and watering processes, but the growth comes from you. Root my mind in this knowledge and understanding.

Humbly I come and ask that you would produce patience within my husband's heart and mine. Praying for patience (for me and for my husband) is not an easy or desirable request, but nonetheless I ask you for it.

While the apostle Paul was in prison, he wrote to the Ephesians, urging them to walk in a manner worthy of the calling they had received. I humbly echo Paul's urging for my husband. Help him to walk in his calling—to walk in patience, humility, and gentleness. Please continue to show him how to bear with others (especially me) in love.

God, you know the importance of the production of patience in our lives, and you cause its growth—thank you! Not only does this fruit help my husband and me endure trials of many kinds (James 1:2–4), but it also helps unify us as the body of Christ (Ephesians 4:1–3). To you, God, be all the glory.

In Jesus' name, amen.

**Use these pages to journal your thoughts,
write your own prayer, or both.**

Date _____

Day 9
For Pure Kindness

But when the goodness and loving kindness
of God our Savior appeared, he saved us, not
because of works done by us in righteousness,
but according to his own mercy, by the
washing of regeneration and renewal of the
Holy Spirit.

Titus 3:4–5

Thank you, God, that your loving-kindness appeared to save us according to your mercy and not because of anything we've done. Your works are wonderful; we know this full well! How can we measure or fathom the depths of your kindness? Thank you for saving us! Thank you for not leaving us the same, but rather, sanctifying us—producing spiritual fruit that is pure and good. I ask that you would produce kindness in my relationship with my husband. I pray that it would be a deep level of kindness, indicating you being at work in us.

I pray for the soul of my husband, that he would experience your kindness in a real and transformative way. Jesus, I ask for your loving-kindness to appear to him and clothe him throughout his day (Colossians 3:12–13).

There is an assurance and peace that comes when your kindness appears to us because you give it to us according to your own mercy and not by our own merit. We have done nothing to deserve your kindness, and yet you freely offer it to us when we believe.

You kindness is powerful and goes beyond a feeling or emotion. It is fruit that produces change in our souls. A change so real and so deep that it leads us to bear with each other in the good and the bad. God, lead us in your loving-kindness and consume us completely. Let us live and love each other in light of your loving-kindness, Jesus.

In Jesus' name, amen.

Use these pages to journal your thoughts, write your own prayer, or both.

Date _____

53

Day 10
That He Would Fight the Good Fight

But as for you, O man of God, flee these things. Pursue righteousness, godliness, faith, love, steadfastness, gentleness. Fight the good fight of the faith. Take hold of the eternal life to which you were called and about which you made the good confession in the presence of many witnesses.

---

1 Timothy 6:11–12

Thank you, God, for bringing clarity to what we, as believers, should pursue and fight for in this life.

Everywhere I look the world is shouting at me to selfishly pursue whatever I feel, or whatever makes me happy at that moment, no matter the cost. The more I pursue these things, the less I pursue you. Help me to fight! Help us to fight the good fight of faith by pursuing righteousness, godliness, faith, love, steadfastness, and gentleness. On the hard days, help me to know that in you I already have victory (John 16:33).

Father, I ask that you would search the heart of my husband and uproot anything that would become an idol and hinder his fight of faith. Draw him close to you and help him to fight faithfully by fleeing from things that are not of you. I pray that the reality of you and eternity in your presence would fuel his fight. Bring clarity to his mind and his heart. Teach and show him exactly how to pursue righteousness, godliness, faith, love, steadfastness, and gentleness every day.

As his wife and helper, lead me in ways that I can encourage him to fight well and to fight faithfully. Help us to fight the good fight of faith together.

In Jesus' name, amen.

**Use these pages to journal your thoughts,
write your own prayer, or both.**

Date _____

Day 11
For a Vibrant Prayer Life

And this is the confidence that we have toward him, that if we ask anything according to his will he hears us.

---

1 John 5:14

Father God, what a gift and privilege it is to talk and commune with you. Through your son, Jesus, you have torn the veil and given us access to the throne of grace. Thank you! Help me to never lose sight of the wonder and privilege it is to pray and speak with the God of the universe. And thank you that it's not a one-way conversation! You have spoken clearly through your Word and left us the Holy Spirit as our Counselor.

God, I pray that you would not only spark, but enliven my husband's prayer life. Deepen his reliance on you, and compel him to bring his every dream, concern, worry, fear, and victory to you in prayer. I pray that this time of communion with you would become a sacred and familiar place. Help him understand what it means to approach you with confidence in Christ—knowing that he is made righteous and holy because of Christ's sacrifice. Burden his heart for the people in his life who need prayer. Open his eyes to opportunities to pray with and for others throughout his day. I pray that his prayers would be powerful, faith-filled, and Spirit led. Help him to lead and model prayer within our family that is both confident and vulnerable.

Teach me what it means to pray—impress upon my heart its importance and cost. Don't let me grow lazy in my prayer life, and forgive me for the many times I've taken it for granted. I know your grace abounds, but I also know that I need as much face-to-face time with you as possible. Thank you that you hear us when we pray.

In Jesus' name, amen.

Use these pages to journal your thoughts, write your own prayer, or both.

Date _____

61

Day 12
For Our Intimacy

I adjure you, O daughters of Jerusalem, if you find my beloved, that you tell him I am sick with love.

_____

Song of Solomon 5:8

Father, you are a relational God. You designed me to know and be known by you. Thank you for creating me in your image, with the capacity to experience and desire you daily. You are the ultimate prize—the only worthy pursuit in life! You're the only source of true satisfaction and complete joy. While you have created me to ultimately glorify and worship you, you have also given me the desire and need for human relationship here on earth. In the beginning you created Adam and said it was not good for him to be alone, so you created and gave him Eve. Together they lived, loved, and were fully known by each other. In the same way, you created my husband and me to live, love, and be fully known by each other.

I ask that you help us to know each other more fully through deeper physical intimacy in our marriage. Help my husband see and value sex the way you do. While I know it's important for me to engage and to desire him, I pray that you begin a work in his heart that gives him a deeper sense of its importance in our marriage. I pray that he would desire me and I would desire him—that we would be "sick with love" for one another as Solomon wrote. Then, I pray that when we're intimate it would glorify you and strengthen our bond as husband and wife.

God, let our physical intimacy be an indication of our emotional closeness and lifelong covenant with each other. Help us to serve each other's physical needs with purity, selflessness, and love. Thank you for the gift of sex. It is good, just as you created it to be! Grow us in this area, and help us to love each other with pure intention and total transparency.

In Jesus' name, amen.

Use these pages to journal your thoughts, write your own prayer, or both.

Date _____

Day 13
For the Freedom to Forgive

And whenever you stand praying, forgive, if you have anything against anyone, so that your Father also who is in heaven may forgive you your trespasses.

Mark 11:25

I praise and thank you, Jesus, for coming to earth and shattering sin's hold on our souls through your life, death, and resurrection. Even in the hours leading up to your unjust and brutal death, you willingly fulfilled the Father's will, resulting in forgiveness of sin for all mankind; reconciling us back to him. You rescued us from being held captive to sin by showing us how to forgive. How deep your love is for us—to provide forgiveness of sins that we had yet to still commit. You knew the depth of my sin and yet you still chose to die (Romans 5:6). You brought forgiveness and freedom to us who would chose slavery and sin. By taking our place you gave us hope, peace, identity, and security in you. From here you call us to forgive.

Holy Spirit, I ask that you would please empower my husband and me to forgive each other as well as those around us. Help us to understand the depths of our own forgiveness both in you and by you.

I ask you, God, to help my husband see any areas or relationships where he has not offered forgiveness. Soften his heart and lead him to freedom through forgiveness. May he understand the grace and forgiveness you provided through Jesus. Help him to let go of whatever is holding him back from forgiving. Whether it be relinquishing control of the situation or stepping out in faith when he is more comfortable ignoring it—empower him, Holy Spirit! Be his rock and equip him with strength (Psalm 18:32). Secure his steps; make wide the path beneath his feet (Psalm 18:36). Make his feet like the deer—able and secure to navigate the heights and potentially fear-filled places that he might need to tread on as he offers forgiveness (Psalm 18:33). Build his faith through this process, and help me to support him and remind him of who he is because of you.

In Jesus' powerful name, amen.

**Use these pages to journal your thoughts,
write your own prayer, or both.**

Date _____

Day 14
Rest and Reflect

The LORD is my shepherd; I shall not want. He makes me lie down in green pastures. He leads me beside still waters. He restores my soul.

Psalm 23:1–3

Take time today to rest in who God is. Reflect on the prayers over the past week. Use the space below to record how God has been working in your heart and marriage.

Day 15
For Contentment in Our Finances

But godliness with contentment is great gain. For we brought nothing into the world, and we can take nothing out of it. But if we have food and clothing, we will be content with that. Those who want to get rich fall into temptation and a trap and into many foolish and harmful desires that plunge people into ruin and destruction. For the love of money is a root of all kinds of evil. Some people, eager for money, have wandered from the faith and pierced themselves with many griefs.

1 Timothy 6:6–10 NIV

Faithful Father God, thank you that in you we have everything we need and could ever want. No amount of money can ever satisfy us or bring contentment. Our souls desire and were created for so much more. In our marriage, money will undoubtedly come and go, but your love and grace are eternal. Thank you that we can find contentment in you no matter what our balance sheet says at the end of the month.

I pray for the heart and mind of my husband as he goes out to work and secure finances for our livelihood—may he be free of anxiety and pressure to perform. Remind him and help him to rest in the knowledge that you are our Provider Father God and he is a steward of what you've given us. Please guard him from loving money and uproot any areas where the love of money has placed a grip on his heart. I ask for freedom and life in the areas of his life where money has enslaved him. Holy Spirit, lead him—Father God, assure him of who you are and redeem his heart and mind-set toward money.

As he goes to work, lead me in how I can help him and build him up in you. Help me to find contentment in the things of you and not in our lack. Build our faith and teach us contentment within our finances. Bring us to our knees if we begin to love money and pursue it more than you.

Thank you, Lord Jesus, for showing us contentment in the midst of trial.

In Jesus' name, amen.

Use these pages to journal your thoughts, write your own prayer, or both.

Date _____

Day 16
For Wonder in the Wild

He is the image of the invisible God, the firstborn of all creation. For by him all things were created, in heaven and on earth, visible and invisible, whether thrones or dominions or rulers or authorities—all things were created through him and for him. And he is before all things, and in him all things hold together.

Colossians 1:15–17

When I look out my windows into your beautiful and wild creation, my heart wells up in awe and wonder of who you are! All praise be to you, Father—the One who spoke the earth into being—creating everything from nothing but your words.

You set the changing seasons into motion and created the boundaries of space and time for our good and for your glory! From every microorganism to the highest mountain peaks, your creation shouts your glory and leads me to do the same. My soul remains in eternal awe and wonder anytime I get to be outdoors and in the wild of your creation.

God, I pray that you would lead my husband's heart into the wild. Maybe it's been too long since he was out in your creation—show me where I can make space for him to freely do this. I pray that his soul would be renewed and encouraged through time spent in your creation.

As his wife, help me to serve him and love him by giving him the freedom to go on a hike, a run, a walk, or a swim—something that gets him outside of his daily schedule to convene with you. Take hold of his heart, open his eyes, inspire his mind, and keep him wild and in awe of you.

Thank you, Jesus, for this grace that we can have because of you and through you.

In Jesus' name, amen.

Use these pages to journal your thoughts, write your own prayer, or both.

Date _____

Day 17
For Confidence as Head of Our Household

For the husband is the head of the wife even as Christ is the head of the church, his body, and is himself its Savior.

Ephesians 5:23

God, I praise and thank you for your good and solid design of covenant and how it functions within the roles you've laid out for us in your Word. Thank you for creating my husband as the head of our household—lead me in how I can confidently step into the role of helper as we navigate our day-to-day life. On those days where I try to take on his role as head of our house by making decisions that aren't mine to make, lead me to joyful repentance. May I trust in your design for the roles you've placed us in.

Jesus, please help my husband to understand that you created him to lead and be the head of our household. Help him to understand and find confidence and assurance in the fact that You are the head of him. I pray he wouldn't be burdened by this fact, but that you would prompt him to lead with devotion and consistency. Teach him how to be the head and how to love as Christ loves the church and gave himself up for her (Ephesians 5:25).

Selflessly I ask you to soften his heart and show him how to love me as he loves his own body (Ephesians 5:28). I ask not for myself, but for the good of his soul and his relationship with you. Help me to die to any desires to take control at the helm of our marriage. Instead, show me how to love him well by letting him lead and begin to confidently step into the role as the head of us.

In your name I ask all these things, amen.

Use these pages to journal your thoughts, write your own prayer, or both.

Date _____

Day 18
For Freedom and Self-Control

For God gave us a spirit not of fear but of
power and love and self-control.

---

2 Timothy 1:7

God, you are always so good to us. Help me as I walk through this prayer of asking for self-control, not only for my husband, but also for myself. It's not an easy or comfortable request, but I petition you, Holy Spirit, to produce and grow this holy fruit in our lives. Help us to throw off any sin that might entangle us (Hebrews 12:1) and choke the life out of the fruit you're producing in us. Lead, guide, and produce a harvest of self-control in our lives—not to restrict our joy, but to deepen it.

In this moment, Holy Spirit, I humbly ask you for the fruit of self-control to be produced in the heart, mind, and soul of my husband. This world we live in would have him live enslaved to every whim, desire, and temptation—to live without boundaries or control. Lord, your ways are higher! You desire freedom for him; even more than he does for himself right now. May your Word remind him that it is for freedom Christ came (Galatians 5:1). Help him to stand firm and use his freedom and life in you as an opportunity to love and serve those around him.

Help him to put to death any desire to serve the flesh. God, I ask you to clearly lead him into your higher way of self-control no matter the situation. Help him to stand firm in your love by being self-controlled—dying to any fleshly desires to burst out in anger or dwell on an impure image; wherever the struggle, I pray he would be met with freedom, confidence, and grace.

Thank you, God, that you have given us a spirit of love, power, and of self-control. May we keep in step with the Spirit in order to glorify you with every breath you've given us.

In Jesus' name, amen.

Use these pages to journal your thoughts, write your own prayer, or both.

Date _____

Day 19
As He Runs His Race

Do you not know that in a race all the runners run, but only one receives the prize? So run that you may obtain it. Every athlete exercises self-control in all things. They do it to receive a perishable wreath, but we an imperishable. So I do not run aimlessly; I do not box as one beating the air.

1 Corinthians 9:24–26

God, you bring purpose and meaning to my every breath. It's by your grace and through your love that I can freely commune with you. May my words, actions, and attitudes be glorifying to you, and may the motivations of my heart make you glad. I know I'm not perfect, which is why I'm forever grateful for your grace! Refine me and make me holy, for my good and your glory.

Thank you for my amazing husband! Thank you for putting him in my life and using him to help sharpen me and remind me of who I am in you. Lord, I pray that you'd fill him with faith today. Help him to understand fully the race he is running. I realize that it's easy for him to lose perspective—just like it's easy for me—and that the daily grind of life can make him weary. I pray that you'd renew my husband and enliven his faith. Remind him that he is your son and a citizen of your everlasting kingdom (Philippians 3:20). Let his ultimate prize be you, Jesus! Give him self-control in all things, and let his every action and word be well aimed. Stir his affections for you, and refresh his appreciation of your grace and goodness.

God, as my husband runs the race you have for him, make his feet swift and his heart strong. Open his eyes to how powerful you are! Give him faith to ask big things of you. Give him faith to speak boldly in love. And give him faith to say no to good things because he is pursuing your absolute best. I love him with all my heart, God. Help me to build him up with words of encouragement and faith. Help me to submit to him well as I remember the race I am in and that you, too, are my ultimate prize.

In Jesus' name, amen.

Use these pages to journal your thoughts, write your own prayer, or both.

Date _____

Day 20
For Assurance in Purpose

Many are the plans in the mind of a man, but it is the purpose of the Lord that will stand.

Proverbs 19:21

Sovereign Lord, I praise you and thank you that you created us in your image and with a purpose that can only be fulfilled in and through you. It is all by your grace that we breathe, work, live, and exist. When we find ourselves in moments of striving and self-reliance, may we be reminded of your steadfast love and promises—assuring us daily that our purpose and eternity are already complete in you.

God, I pray that my husband would find his worth, identity, and purpose in you. As he makes plans for our life together, I pray that each of those plans would be anchored in you and held with an open hand and open mind. Let him rest assured that even if he makes these plans, ultimately it is your purpose that will stand. In a world that would live distracted and without purpose, I pray that you would give him wisdom to number his days (Psalm 90:12) in order to live assuredly in your purpose for his life. I ask that if there is pride or ambition that is blinding him from the purposes you have for him, you would open his eyes and heart and lead him back to you.

It is easy for our hearts to fall away from you and to search for meaning and purpose in distractions. All too often we let our desires and passions have the final say in our decisions. I pray this would not be so in the heart of my husband (and myself). May we remember that we are your workmanship, created in Christ Jesus for good works, which you prepared beforehand that we should walk in them (Ephesians 2:10). Above all, teach us to rest in the assurance of our purpose in you.

In Jesus' name, amen.

Use these pages to journal your thoughts, write your own prayer, or both.

Date _____

97

Day 21
Rest and Reflect

You keep him in perfect peace whose mind is stayed on you, because he trusts in you.

Isaiah 26:3

Take time today to rest in who God is. Reflect on the prayers over the past week. Use the space below to record how God has been working in your heart and marriage.

Day 22
For Reconciliation

All this is from God, who through Christ reconciled us to himself and gave us the ministry of reconciliation; that is, in Christ God was reconciling the world to himself, not counting their trespasses against them, and entrusting to us the message of reconciliation.

2 Corinthians 5:18–19

Lord, please help me to identify areas needing reconciliation in my marriage. Open my eyes to these areas, large or small. I want unity within our covenant. Unity begins with reconciliation. Lead me, Father. I praise you and thank you for being the author of reconciliation. While we were still sinners, you chose to die so that we could be made new and reconciled back to the Father (Romans 5:8). My sin didn't stop you and death couldn't hold you—praise God! My heart finds assurance in the fact that nothing is out of your control and that you are fully aware of the struggles my marriage is facing at this moment. Help us, God. Lead us down your path of reconciliation and righteousness.

Help us, Holy Spirit, to not live from our own strength or knowledge, but rather, teach us how to live from a place of knowing who we are in Christ because of what he's done. From here, lead my husband and me in our words and actions as we ask for clarity on this path of reconciliation.

Soften our hearts; open our ears—help us to fight off our fleshly urges to lash out in anger or fight to be right. Lead us in your higher ways of love, and help us to hear what each other is trying to communicate. Empower us, Holy Spirit, to extend grace to each other and to relinquish control or the desire to be right. Help us to love each other well, even as we take this first step toward reconciling. Let fear fall at the foot of the cross.

In Jesus' name, amen.

Use these pages to journal your thoughts, write your own prayer, or both.

Date _____

Day 23
That He Would Be a Warrior

Finally, be strong in the Lord and in his mighty power. Put on the full armor of God, so that you can take your stand against the devil's schemes.

Ephesians 6:10–11 NIV

Lord, this world is stained with sin, and even when we try to live peaceably with all (Romans 12:18), we will undoubtedly be faced with times of battle. Help us in these moments, God. Lead and prepare us in all wisdom and strength to not back down, but to stand firm in the gospel when everything in and around us would have us compromise.

Raise up the warrior spirit within my husband! As his wife, I pray that you would prepare him for the battles he will face, both spiritually and in the natural realm. Thank you that your Word is clear and empowering. May we be reminded that the battles we fight are not against flesh and blood, but against spiritual forces of evil in heavenly places (Ephesians 6:12). I humbly ask that you would make clear to him the battles he should engage in and how to wisely fight with you as his rock!

I pray he would put on the whole armor that you provide, that he may be able to stand against the schemes of the enemy (Ephesians 6:11). Help him to be sober-minded and watchful as the enemy prowls around, seeking ways to devour him (1 Peter 5:8). I pray that in all circumstances he would take up his shield of faith in order to extinguish all the flaming darts of the evil one. I pray that he would cover his head with the helmet of salvation and hold firm in his hand the sword of the Spirit, which is your Word (Ephesians 6:10–17). Lord, be his rock—train his hands for war and his fingers for battle. Please, Jesus, be his confidence and his strength in the trials you said we would face.

May we count these trials as sources of joy, knowing that the testing of our faith produces steadfastness (James 1:2–4).

In Jesus' name, amen.

Use these pages to journal your thoughts, write your own prayer, or both.

Date _____

Day 24
For Renewed Hope

Why are you cast down, O my soul, and why are you in turmoil within me? Hope in God; for I shall again praise him, my salvation. . . . By day the Lᴏʀᴅ commands his steadfast love, and at night his song is with me, a prayer to the God of my life.

Psalm 42:5, 8

God, thank you for this gift of life. Every day is different in that every trial faced is a unique reminder of your goodness, your sovereignty and grace. I am so undeserving—but that's why it's called grace. My heart overflows with gratefulness. Even in the darkest and heaviest of moments, you remain faithful and present. You remind me that you will never leave or forsake me; your steadfast love sustains me. My hope is renewed.

I pray for the heart of my husband as he faces each day and the joys and trials that come with it. May the joy he experiences remind him of your goodness as our Father, and may the trials he faces be opportunities for renewed hope in you.

The weight of this world is crushing, but your burden is light—God, please remind him of this truth! When he feels the weight of this world, I pray your love would sustain him and renew his hope in you.

Help me, as his wife, to comfort and co-travel with him. May I encourage him in your truth and the reality of who you are in the midst of any turmoil he is feeling and facing. Help me to be the helper you desire for me to be in this situation. Thank you that you hear our prayers and you lead us in love, renewing our hope in you at every turn.

In Jesus' name, amen.

Use these pages to journal your thoughts, write your own prayer, or both.

Date _____

Day 25
For Unity in the Midst of Transitions

Make every effort to keep the unity of the Spirit through the bond of peace.

Ephesians 4:3 NIV

Thank you, Jesus, that you are the same yesterday, today, and forever. You're steadfast, trustworthy, and our Rock no matter the life transitions we will undoubtedly face in our marriage. I pray that you would unify our souls and lead us in peace. Let this time of transition be an opportunity for us to grow closer to you and in turn, closer to each other. Help us to live a life worthy of the calling we've received—being humble, gentle, and patient with each other, bearing with one another in love while walking this unfamiliar path.

As we face the unfamiliar ahead, I pray specifically for my husband to remain soft, vulnerable, and transparent with me about how he is feeling about the unknown. Please help me, God, to be a safe harbor for him to voice his feelings and to process any fears or anxieties that might creep in. Build his faith through the trials that unfamiliarity undoubtedly brings. Walking from here to there can create so much fear and anxiety—I ask that the peace of Christ would rule our hearts and unify our souls (Colossians 3:15).

May our thankfulness grow as we learn to settle into our new season of life. We ask that this season of transition would be an opportunity for us to create new rhythms and habits that would lead us to abide in you. I ask that you would help us to quickly find a gospel community where we can grow and be known by people who care about us and who want to see us grow deeper in our faith and understanding of the gospel.

In Jesus' name, amen.

**Use these pages to journal your thoughts,
write your own prayer, or both.**

Date _____

Day 26
That He Would Be a Peacemaker

Do not be anxious about anything, but in everything by prayer and supplication with thanksgiving let your requests be made known to God. And the peace of God, which surpasses all understanding, will guard your hearts and your minds in Christ Jesus.

Philippians 4:6–7

By your grace, Father, you created us to be image bearers—made in your likeness to reflect your character and bring you glory. When anxiety creeps in to disturb the peace you freely give, I praise and thank you for remaining present, for never leaving or forsaking us. No matter the magnitude of the storms we find ourselves in, you faithfully stand with us—rebuking the waves and commanding "peace" and stillness (Mark 4:39).

God, I pray for the heart, mind, soul, and body of my husband to be flooded with your peace that surpasses understanding. Let it guard his heart and his mind in Christ Jesus (Philippians 4:6–7). Let it fill him so completely that it spills over into every aspect of his world. Holy Spirit, when his mind is troubled and his heart feels uneasy, be the one to bring him back to you. Finally, I pray that he be known by his coworkers and his family members because of the otherworldly, inexplicable peace you've given him and lead him to share with others.

In moments of confusion and confrontation, I pray that he would be uncompromising in his promotion of peace within the situation. Holy Spirit, I ask you to give him words and wisdom in how to speak and how to act in such a way that brings you glory and reflects your character. Continue molding my husband into the peacemaker you desire for our marriage, our home, and in this world. All praise and glory to you, God!

In Jesus' name, amen.

Use these pages to journal your thoughts, write your own prayer, or both.

Date _____

Day 27
For Righteous Desires

Delight yourself in the LORD, and he will give you the desires of your heart.

Psalm 37:4

Thank you, God, for sanctifying our hearts and in turn our desires when we accept Jesus and believe in the work he did to reconcile us back into relationship with you. Jesus changes everything! All the way down to the deepest desires of our hearts. Father, I pray that you would teach us daily what it means to delight in you, in your Word, and in your ways.

Father, I ask for the purification, sanctification, and in turn, transformation of the desires in my husband's heart. If there are desires that are lustful or impure, I pray that you would help him (and us) to identify them in order to bring restoration to your master design for our marriage. Lead me in grace and wisdom in the role you desire me to play in this process. In faith I ask you for his sexual desire to be for me—his wife, and for no one else.

I pray for the temptation that my husband faces on a daily basis. Not only sexually, but also the temptation to live pridefully or without self-control or discipline. Truly it is our sinful desires that lead us into temptation, sin, and ultimately death (James 1:14). Transform his desires, from the core of his being, to be from you and to reflect you. I pray that his desires would be your desires and that he would find delight and joy in you. Help him to seek first your kingdom and your righteousness (Matthew 6:33).

Help me, Lord, and show me how I can love him well and encourage him in his newfound desires from you.

In Jesus' name, amen.

Use these pages to journal your thoughts, write your own prayer, or both.

Date _____

Day 28
Rest and Reflect

In peace I will both lie down and sleep; for you alone, O LORD, make me dwell in safety.

Psalm 4:8

Take time today to rest in who God is. Reflect on the prayers over the past week. Use the space below to record how God has been working in your heart and marriage.

Day 29
For a Deep Love for Scripture

Your word is a lamp to my feet and a light to my path.

Psalm 119:105

Thank you, God, for your Word, which is alive, active, and sharper than any double-edged sword. What else penetrates even to dividing soul and spirit, joints and marrow, and judges the thoughts and attitudes of the heart (Hebrews 4:12)? Truly, there is no other book that provides a greater message of hope, freedom, grace, and love than the Bible.

God, I ask that you would deepen my husband's love for your Word. Even if he doesn't feel like reading the Bible, I pray that he would remain devoted to your Word. Help him to trust the power of Scripture over his own feelings. Teach and solidify in him the value of knowing, memorizing, and storing your Word in his heart. May he understand the person and work of Jesus through the Scriptures. I pray that he would see your Word as a way of him guarding his way and keeping it pure. Help him to find joy and delight in storing up your Word in his heart through memorization and daily encounters with you in prayer (Psalm 119:11). Nothing else in this world can compare to the power of Scripture.

As his wife I ask you to also deepen my love for your Word. May this be a place that we can grow in together and share with each other what you're teaching us. Guide us, through your Word, and may we come to value the Scriptures above anything in this world. What a gift to be able to read your Word freely—and to let it read us. May it be the authority we answer to, the road map we look to, and the source of strength we cling to every day.

In Jesus' name, amen.

**Use these pages to journal your thoughts,
write your own prayer, or both.**

Date _____

Day 30
For Humility Through Christ

Do nothing from selfish ambition or conceit, but in humility count others more significant than yourselves.

Philippians 2:3

Thank you, Jesus, for dying on the cross and emptying yourself for us while we were still sinners. You could have laid claim to your identity as King and displayed your power as God—but instead you chose humility and obedience, even to death on a cross (Philippians 2:8). You did this so that we could be found complete in you and through you. Teach us to live in light of what you achieved for us. May our hearts be filled with joy and humility because of your life, Jesus.

If I am honest, Lord, at some level it feels wrong to pray for humility in my husband. It's not that I am above this or have achieved success in terms of my humility; so please help my heart as I ask you for humility—keep my motives pure, God.

God, I ask that you would deepen his hunger for understanding you and the things of you. I pray that humility would be something he desires and experiences because of Jesus and in light of the gospel. May his encounters with you be full of both gratitude and conviction. Gratitude in knowing that everything he has is by your grace, and conviction if and when he takes pride and exalts himself to the place of god. Remind him that his identity is secure in you. From here, let him see clearly how he can decrease so that you can increase. I pray that he finds joy and completeness in you as he learns how to relinquish himself in order to serve others.

Teach us both about the beauty in humility. May we fix our eyes on Jesus, the ultimate example of humility and obedience. Help us to count others better than ourselves as we understand your definition of humility more every day.

In Jesus' name, amen.

Use these pages to journal your thoughts, write your own prayer, or both.

Date _____

Day 31
For Strength in His Body

Or do you not know that your body is a temple
of the Holy Spirit within you, whom you have
from God? You are not your own, for you were
bought with a price. So glorify God in your
body.

---

1 Corinthians 6:19–20

How wondrous are your works, Lord; we know them full well! Our frames were not hidden from you when we were being made in secret. Your eyes saw me, unformed—and each of my days was formed and written in your book (Psalm 139:15–16). Our physical bodies are a miraculous reflection of our magnificent Creator!

I pray that through my husband's understanding of his body being a temple of you, Holy Spirit, he would steward it well. May he make decisions in light of the fact that he is no longer his own but has been purchased at a price that he could never repay. You created my husband completely and perfectly. Help him to care for himself in a way that displays you as Lord of his life. Be his strength both spiritually and physically. Lead him to right decisions that will aid him in serving you best. Guard his mind against any vain conceit or selfish ambition—lead him in righteousness for your name's sake. Let not sin reign in his mortal body to make it obey its passions (Romans 6:12). Instead, please remind him that he is a new creation in Christ (2 Corinthians 5:17). Teach us how to steward our bodies well out of gratitude to you, Jesus, who made us new.

Please show me how to love, encourage, and partner with him on how we can build our physical strength together for your glory. Help us to come up with a practical plan and implement new rhythms into our weekly schedules so that we may glorify you in our bodies. Purify our motives and make our path clear and full of joy.

In Jesus' name, amen.

Use these pages to journal your thoughts, write your own prayer, or both.

Date _____

Day 32
For Trust in Healing

But he was pierced for our transgressions; he was crushed for our iniquities; upon him was the chastisement that brought us peace, and with his wounds we are healed.

Isaiah 53:5

Thank you, Jesus, for being wounded for our transgressions and crushed for our iniquities—it is by your stripes that we are healed; it is also by your stripes that we can pray and speak directly to you and ask for healing!

Lord, I know that you are more than able to heal my husband of his ailments (spiritually, physically, or mentally), but I also know and trust that your ways are higher than mine. Help me to align and submit (if need be) my ideas and desires of healing to your will. Give me faith, Lord, in this request that feels a bit scary and confusing. Yes, I want my husband to be healed and I want to pray, ask, and believe in faith! But I also long for a soft heart if the healing I'm asking and believing for is denied. Teach us how to trust you in this request and in your answer. Lead us in truth, Jesus, and give us faith to believe that even if your answer to our healing of a physical ailment is no, you are still a good Father and sovereign King.

Help us to trust you and not lean on our own understanding. To not be wise in our own eyes but to acknowledge you and turn from evil. Your Word says that this will bring healing to our flesh and refreshment to our bones (Proverbs 3:5–8). I pray for your healing from sin, physical ailments, spiritual and mental ailments. You are Jehovah Rapha, the Lord Our Healer.

No matter your response, God, we still will come, as children to a Father, requesting what you can and are fully able to give, all the while trusting your providential nature and goodness.

In Jesus' name, amen.

Use these pages to journal your thoughts, write your own prayer, or both.

Date _____

Day 33
That He Would Fight Familiarity

Whatever you do, work at it with all your heart, as working for the Lord, not for human masters, since you know that you will receive an inheritance from the Lord as a reward. It is the Lord Christ you are serving.

Colossians 3:23–24 NIV

Father God, I praise and thank you for who you are. Your very nature offers us reconciliation, transformation, and in turn: new life through Christ! Our lives are blessed beyond anything we could hope for or imagine simply because we are your children.

I pray for my husband right now as he may be struggling with feeling as though his life is lackluster and burdensome. As the enemy prowls around, I ask that my husband would be alert and sober-minded (1 Peter 5:8)—not so familiar with this life that he would desire "more" and be tempted away from you, Lord. I ask that you would be his strength, his life, and his hope! In his life rhythms and perspective, I ask that he would not be conformed to the pattern of this world, but that he would be transformed by the renewing of his mind through your Word. Give him profound joy in the work he does, especially when familiarity would push him to respond with indifference or ungratefulness; I ask you, Holy Spirit, to help him combat these responses that he could so easily fall into. Equip him to battle well!

Let us only become familiar with you, Jesus—and the new creation we are in you and because of you. When we forget the good news of the gospel and become too consumed with our lives and our own selfish desires, lead us back to repentance and bring our hearts back to the foot of the cross. May we fight off familiarity that would lead us to sin, by knowing that we are a new creation and free to love and live selflessly for Christ.

In Jesus' name, amen.

Use these pages to journal your thoughts, write your own prayer, or both.

Date _____

Day 34
For Soul Rest

"Come to me, all you who are weary and burdened, and I will give you rest. Take my yoke upon you and learn from me, for I am gentle and humble in heart, and you will find rest for your souls. For my yoke is easy and my burden is light."

Matthew 11:28–30 NIV

Thank you, God, for being our source for true soul rest. Every day we struggle with feeling weary and burdened, for so many reasons. Even still, you faithfully invite us to take your easy yoke and to learn from you. Help us to know you so that we may learn from you.

Lord, my husband's soul needs the kind of rest that only comes from knowing you through being in relationship with you. In the midst of his day-to-day schedule, I pray that he would know you deeply and see you at work in his world. If and when he finds himself striving for things that only you can give, I ask that you would please lead him back to you. In your presence I pray that he would find all the security, acceptance, and rest he needs and desires. Help him to experience and differentiate between temporary rest that might come from sleep, self-care, or hobbies—and soul rest that comes from you and requires nothing from us but to simply rest.

Reassure his soul to be still and to know that you are God (Psalm 46:10). As he moves forward into the hard work of being a husband, father, brother, son, coworker, friend—I pray that your nature and presence would be his soul's source of rest.

As his wife, lead me in how I can help him find rest in you.

In Jesus' name, amen.

Use these pages to journal your thoughts, write your own prayer, or both.

Date _____

Day 35
Rest and Reflect

Then, because so many people were coming and going that they did not even have a chance to eat, he said to them, "Come with me by yourselves to a quiet place and get some rest."

Mark 6:31 NIV

Take time today to rest in who God is. Reflect on the prayers over the past week. Use the space below to record how God has been working in your heart and marriage.

Day 36
For Redeemed Joy

My lips will shout for joy, when I sing praises to you; my soul also, which you have redeemed.

Psalm 71:23

Jesus, thank you for being our redeemer. By your blood we are reconciled and redeemed—may our souls never cease to rejoice in you (1 Thessalonians 5:16). As Mary sang out when she was pregnant with you, Jesus, "My soul magnifies the Lord, and my spirit rejoices in God my Savior" (Luke 1:46–47), so also my soul sings out with joy and gladness!

God, I pray for my husband's joy to be found in you every day. I pray that his lips would shout for joy and his soul would sing praises to you because you love him, you're drawing him near to you, and you have redeemed him! I ask that his hope in you would produce a joy renewed and anchored in you completely. When he is faced with times of despair, anxiety, or hopelessness, I pray that he would be reminded of your goodness and your faithfulness. I ask that gratefulness for all you have given him would flood his heart and mind, and the joy produced from knowing you would cause his soul to shout and sing praises to you!

Truly you are faithful and good—never abandoning us or forsaking us; even in the midst of our sin. What a hope we have in you! All praise and glory to you, Jesus, redeemer of our joy!

In Jesus' name, amen.

Use these pages to journal your thoughts, write your own prayer, or both.

Date _____

_____

_____

_____

_____

_____

_____

_____

_____

_____

_____

_____

_____

_____

_____

_____

_____

_____

_____

_____

_____

_____

_____

_____

161

Day 37
That He Would Believe God Is Enough

"Blessed are those who hunger and thirst for righteousness, for they will be filled."

Matthew 5:6 NIV

God, I praise you and thank you for who you are. Sometimes we struggle with allowing you to simply be enough for us. We look around for something or someone else to be our fill, and in your grace and kindness, you allow our idols to be smashed. In our brokenness and sin, our souls quickly forget all that you have done, and our hunger intensifies. Help us, Jesus.

Help my husband in his belief that you are enough for him. Help him to stand firm in the faith you've given him, and I ask that you would lead and guide him to hunger for you more than anything or anyone else. Truly you are all that we need and there is nothing outside of you that our souls need. And yet, I know he struggles. If I am honest, I too struggle with this fact. In the midst of the trials, struggles, and difficulties he faces, there is an enemy tempting him to rely on himself and his own abilities. I pray against this temptation and ask that he would be reminded of how you struggled for forty days in the desert. When the enemy appealed to your abilities, you spoke out and answered him, "Man shall not live by bread alone, but by every word that comes from the mouth of God" (Matthew 4:4). I pray that my husband's hunger for you would lead him to Scripture and empower him.

All too often our eyes and hearts are drawn to the lack that we see in and around our lives. In those moments, may we be reminded that we do not live by bread alone, but by every word that comes from your mouth, Father God. Thank you, God, that you are enough. Lead us in this knowledge and truth as a married couple.

In Jesus' name, amen.

**Use these pages to journal your thoughts,
write your own prayer, or both.**

Date _____

Day 38
That He Would Be Salt and Light

"You are the salt of the earth, but if salt has lost its taste, how shall its saltiness be restored? It is no longer good for anything except to be thrown out and trampled under people's feet. You are the light of the world. A city set on a hill cannot be hidden."

Matthew 5:13–14

Father God, hallowed be your name! Thank you for being our loving Father, who sent his Son as a sacrifice for us (Romans 8:32). Jesus, thank you for coming to earth to fulfill the law and to teach us how to live in a way that illuminates you in our everyday lives. In your kindness you teach and show us the way to abundant life that is only found in and through you (John 10:10). Thank you that, while we are in the world, we are not of the world. We are salt and light because of you, Jesus. Guide us in this.

God, I ask that you would embolden my husband to continually be salt and light both in our home and outside of it. I pray that he would be a city on a hill, unhidden and humble—all the while illuminating Jesus everywhere he goes. Grow him in his faith; help him to return to Scripture over and over and over so he may be reminded of who you are. This in turn reminds him of who he is in light of you. Root his identity in you and empower him to shine bright as a beacon of hope because of you.

As his wife, help me to encourage him and love him well. Lead and guide me in your words through Scripture, that I too would abide in you and be salt and light to those inside and outside our home. Thank you for all you have done and are doing in our lives. Draw us closer to you and make our hearts attentive to your will and your ways.

In Jesus' name, amen.

Use these pages to journal your thoughts, write your own prayer, or both.

Date _____

169

Day 39
For Perseverance

Blessed is the man who remains steadfast under trial, for when he has stood the test he will receive the crown of life, which God has promised to those who love him.

James 1:12

Thank you, Jesus, for overcoming the world! When you spoke to your disciples, warning them about the trials they would face because of you, you also reminded them that you have overcome the world (John 16:33). My heart is grateful and humbled to be loved and called by the Savior of the world. Our trials are temporary, but you are eternal!

God, I pray that my husband's hope would be anchored in you. Help him to lean into the fact that nothing can separate him from you or your love (Romans 8:38–39). Because of your love for us, we are saved and brought into relationship with you. I pray that in his communion with you he would continue learning what it means to persevere under trial. The trials he faces can feel crushing and overwhelming—help him to abide in you. Reveal your presence to him and remind him to not be afraid but to take courage (Deuteronomy 31:6). Jesus, I ask that you would be his strength and his hope—help him to remain steadfast under trial and to cling to your promise to receive the crown of life given to those who love you. I pray that he would not grow weary in doing good, but that he would cling to you and your promise of reaping and receiving in your timing (Galatians 6:9).

It is in you that we are able to persevere through the darkest of days.

In Jesus' name, amen.

Use these pages to journal your thoughts, write your own prayer, or both.

Date _____

173

Day 40
For Willingness to Be Known

But if we walk in the light, as he is in the light, we have fellowship with one another, and the blood of Jesus his Son cleanses us from all sin.

_____

1 John 1:7

Thank you, God, for being light!

Your Word reminds us that there is no darkness in you—none! Jesus came so that we could be reconciled, redeemed, and freed from the darkness and the sin that so easily entangles us (Hebrews 12:1).

I pray for my husband and the sin and darkness he may want to hide from me and from those in our gospel community. Lovingly lead him to you, Jesus. Thank you, God, that you have not given him a spirit of fear, but of love, power, and self-control (2 Timothy 1:7). Please remind him of this. I pray that he would experience your fullness of grace in the midst of his sin and struggle. Lead him back to the cross—that he would cast down his fear and anxiety there.

Give him the courage to be fully known and to know that he is fully loved no matter the sin and darkness that he struggles with this side of glory. As his love for you grows, I pray that his desire to walk in the light would grow. Create in him a desire to be fully known first by you, then by me, and then by our gospel community.

Lead me, Holy Spirit, as I learn to love him in this fragile place of being known. Those first steps into the light can be frightening, but not impossible. Give him courage to know that the deep, dark sin he is hiding is the very one that Jesus died for. I pray that you would fill him with hope and freedom as he learns to be known. May his desire to be fully known joyfully and organically increase because of you. All glory and praise be to you, God! As long as we live, may we sing praises to you (Psalm 146:1).

In Jesus' name, amen.

Use these pages to journal your thoughts, write your own prayer, or both.

Date _____

At Journey's End

I hope you've experienced God's grace and faithfulness in new and transformative ways over the past forty days. Spend a few minutes answering the questions below and reflecting on your experience through this book.

How has God moved in your husband's heart over the past forty days? How has he transformed your marriage? Be specific.

Have you changed as a woman and as a wife? How?

How has your faith grown? Try to list three specific ways.

Now that you're finished with this book, how will you intentionally pray for your husband?

Knowing what you know now, how will you love your family by praying for them and with them?

Turn back to page 15 and rate the aspects of your marriage once again. What are the most significant changes?

50 Verses on Prayer

Sometimes we need to be reminded of what the Bible says about prayer. This list of verses is not exhaustive, and each one is part of a greater context. As you read the verses below, note the ones that jump out at you; then read your Bible for surrounding context. Doing so will give you a more thorough understanding of prayer's role and importance in your life.

Rejoice always, pray without ceasing, give thanks in all circumstances; for this is the will of God in Christ Jesus for you.

1 Thessalonians 5:16–18

Do not be anxious about anything, but in everything by prayer and supplication with thanksgiving let your requests be made known to God. And the peace of God, which surpasses all understanding, will guard your hearts and your minds in Christ Jesus.

Philippians 4:6–7

And this is the confidence that we have toward him, that if we ask anything according to his will he hears us.

1 John 5:14

Continue steadfastly in prayer, being watchful in it with thanksgiving.

Colossians 4:2

"Therefore I tell you, whatever you ask in prayer, believe that you have received it, and it will be yours."

Mark 11:24

"Then you will call upon me and come and pray to me, and I will hear you."

Jeremiah 29:12

Rejoice in hope, be patient in tribulation, be constant in prayer.

Romans 12:12

"And when you pray, do not heap up empty phrases as the Gentiles do, for they think that they will be heard for their many words."

Matthew 6:7

The LORD is near to all who call on him,
to all who call on him in truth.

Psalm 145:18

"Call to me and I will answer you, and will tell you great and hidden things that you have not known."

Jeremiah 33:3

"For where two or three are gathered in my name, there am I among them."

Matthew 18:20

Let us then with confidence draw near to the throne of grace, that we may receive mercy and find grace to help in time of need.

Hebrews 4:16

"But when you pray, go into your room and shut the door and pray to your Father who is in secret. And your Father who sees in secret will reward you."

Matthew 6:6

In my distress I called upon the Lord; to my God I cried for help. From his temple he heard my voice, and my cry to him reached his ears.

Psalm 18:6

And if we know that he hears us in whatever we ask, we know that we have the requests that we have asked of him.

1 John 5:15

But let him ask in faith, with no doubting, for the one who doubts is like a wave of the sea that is driven and tossed by the wind.

James 1:6

Therefore, confess your sins to one another and pray for one another, that you may be healed. The prayer of a righteous person has great power as it is working.

James 5:16

"But I say to you who hear, love your enemies, do good to those who hate you, bless those who curse you, pray for those who abuse you."

Luke 6:27–28

About midnight Paul and Silas were praying and singing hymns to God, and the prisoners were listening to them.

Acts 16:25

All these with one accord were devoting themselves to prayer, together with the women and Mary the mother of Jesus, and his brothers.

Acts 1:14

The end of all things is at hand; therefore be self-controlled and sober-minded for the sake of your prayers.

1 Peter 4:7

"You did not choose me, but I chose you and appointed you that you should go and bear fruit and that your fruit should abide, so that whatever you ask the Father in my name, he may give it to you."

John 15:16

"Whatever you ask in my name, this I will do, that the Father may be glorified in the Son."

John 14:13

I cried to him with my mouth,
and high praise was on my tongue.

Psalm 66:17

You desire and do not have, so you murder. You covet and cannot obtain, so you fight and quarrel. You do not have, because you do not ask.

James 4:2

Likewise the Spirit helps us in our weakness. For we do not know what to pray for as we ought, but the Spirit himself intercedes for us with groanings too deep for words.

Romans 8:26

"And whatever you ask in prayer, you will receive, if you have faith."

Matthew 21:22

Out of my distress I called on the LORD;
the LORD answered me and set me free.

Psalm 118:5

For I know that through your prayers and the help of the Spirit of Jesus Christ this will turn out for my deliverance.

Philippians 1:19

O LORD, in the morning you hear my voice;
in the morning I prepare a sacrifice for you and watch.

Psalm 5:3

By day the LORD commands his steadfast love, and at night his song is with me, a prayer to the God of my life.

Psalm 42:8

"If you then, who are evil, know how to give good gifts to your children, how much more will the heavenly Father give the Holy Spirit to those who ask him!"

Luke 11:13

Let the words of my mouth and the meditation of my heart be acceptable in your sight, O LORD, my rock and my redeemer.

Psalm 19:14

Beloved, I pray that all may go well with you and that you may be in good health, as it goes well with your soul.

3 John 2

Hear my prayer, O LORD; give ear to my pleas for mercy!
In your faithfulness answer me, in your righteousness!

Psalm 143:1

"But I say to you, Love your enemies and pray for those who persecute you."

Matthew 5:44

"Father, I desire that they also, whom you have given me, may be with me where I am, to see my glory that you have given me because you loved me before the foundation of the world."

John 17:24

Then after fasting and praying they laid their hands on them and sent them off.

Acts 13:3

And taking the five loaves and the two fish, he looked up to heaven and said a blessing over them. Then he broke the loaves and gave them to the disciples to set before the crowd. And they all ate and were satisfied. And what was left over was picked up, twelve baskets of broken pieces.

Luke 9:16–17

"I made known to them your name, and I will continue to make it known, that the love with which you have loved me may be in them, and I in them."

John 17:26

Arise, O Lord; O God, lift up your hand;
  forget not the afflicted.

Psalm 10:12

For the eyes of the Lord are on the righteous,
  and his ears are open to their prayer.
But the face of the Lord is against those who do evil.

1 Peter 3:12

To you, O God of my fathers, I give thanks and praise, for you have given me wisdom and might, and have now made known to me what we asked of you, for you have made known to us the king's matter.

Daniel 2:23

Is anyone among you sick? Let him call for the elders of the church, and let them pray over him, anointing him with oil in the name of the Lord. And the prayer of faith will save the one who is sick, and the Lord will raise him up. And if he has committed sins, he will be forgiven.

James 5:14–15

"Watch and pray that you may not enter into temptation. The spirit indeed is willing, but the flesh is weak."

Matthew 26:41

"And when you pray, you must not be like the hypocrites. For they love to stand and pray in the synagogues and at the street corners, that they may be seen by others. Truly, I say to you, they have received their reward. But when you pray, go into your room and shut the door and pray to your Father who is in secret. And your Father who sees in secret will reward you. And when you pray, do not heap up empty phrases as the Gentiles do, for they think that they will be heard for their many words. Do not be like them, for your Father knows what you need before you ask him."

Matthew 6:5–8

This poor man cried, and the Lord heard him
  and saved him out of all his troubles.

Psalm 34:6

"Pray then like this: 'Our Father in heaven, hallowed be your name. Your kingdom come, your will be done, on earth as it is in heaven. Give us this day our daily bread, and forgive us our debts, as we also have forgiven our debtors. And lead us not into temptation, but deliver us from evil.'"

Matthew 6:9–13

While they were worshiping the Lord and fasting, the Holy Spirit said, "Set apart for me Barnabas and Saul for the work to which I have called them."

Acts 13:2

Now when all the people were baptized, and when Jesus also had been baptized and was praying, the heavens were opened, and the Holy Spirit descended on him in bodily form, like a dove; and a voice came from heaven, "You are my beloved Son; with you I am well pleased."

Luke 3:21–22

"Turn back, and say to Hezekiah the leader of my people, Thus says the Lord, the God of David your father: I have heard your prayer; I have seen your tears. Behold, I will heal you. On the third day you shall go up to the house of the Lord."

2 Kings 20:5

Additional Resources

You are reading a Fierce Marriage resource. Fierce Marriage exists to point couples to Christ and commission marriages for the gospel. That one mission drives everything we do, this book included. In addition, we produce content daily via our podcast, blog, and on social media.

The Fierce Marriage Podcast

Listen in every week as Ryan and Selena discuss modern marriage issues in light of the gospel. Subscribe and listen on iTunes, Spotify, or anywhere else podcasts are found.

Find Us Online

Website: FierceMarriage.com
Email: FierceMarriage.com/List
Facebook: /FierceMarriage
Instagram: @FierceMarriage
YouTube: /FierceMarriage
Twitter: @FierceMarriage

Recommended Books

For a list of books we love and recommend, visit FierceMarriage.com/Resources.

Share This Book with a Friend

If you'd like to share this book with a friend, please direct them to 40Prayers.com.

Share an Image

Snap a picture of you and your spouse and share it using our hashtags, #40Prayers and #FierceMarriage. We'd love to see your faces and see how our resources are helping you!

Do You Have Feedback or a Story?

If this book has helped you, please share your story with us. If we can improve or fix anything about this resource, please let us know by sending an email to care@fiercemarriage.com.

Want to Leave a Review?

If you've enjoyed this book, we'd be honored if you wrote an honest review wherever you purchased your copy (on our website, Amazon.com, or elsewhere). Make sure to share how God is working in your marriage. You never know who might read it and be encouraged.

Group Study Leaders

If you would like to lead a small group based on this book, bulk discounts are available (8+ copies). Please email details to care@fiercemarriage.com and someone will be in touch.

Speaking Requests

Ryan and Selena are happy to work alongside churches and event organizers to bring gospel-centered hope and help to couples around the world through relatable teaching.

For speaking inquiries, visit FierceMarriage.com/Speaking.

Take the 31-Day Pursuit Challenge

Husband in Pursuit and *Wife in Pursuit* offer a gospel-centered path for couples who want to learn to creatively love each other as Christ has loved them. Over thirty-one days, you and your husband will dive into God's Word, rediscover how Christ has pursued you, and take intentional action to pursue each other.

Take the 31-Day Pursuit Challenge together.

Learn more at **31DayPursuit.com**

A 30-Day Couple's Devotional

Draw closer to God and your husband through thirty daily
devotions, each one brought to life with imagery
and practical application.

Each day starts with an image/quote combination designed to
inspire and stimulate conversation. Explore passages of the
Bible, connect the gospel to real challenges,
and pray alongside your husband.

Learn more at **TwoAsOne.org**

Pray without ceasing.

1 Thessalonians 5:17